I0821762

THE GARDEN

a poem and an essay

A. F. Moritz

Edited by Shane Neilson
Cover and book design by Jeremy Luke Hill
Proofreading by Carol Dilworth
Set in Tenez
Printed on Mohawk Via Felt
Printed and bound by Arkay Design & Print

LIBRARY AND ARCHIVES CANADA CATALOGUING IN PUBLICATION

Title: The garden : a poem and an essay / A.F. Moritz.
Other titles: Works. Selections
Names: Moritz, A. F. (Albert Frank), author. | container of (work): Moritz, A. F. (Albert Frank). Garden in the midst. | container of (work): Moritz, A. F. (Albert Frank). Poet's garden.
Identifiers: Canadiana (print) 20200369865 | Canadiana (ebook) 20200369989 | ISBN 9781774220382 (softcover) | ISBN 9781774220399 (PDF) | ISBN 9781774220405 (HTML)
Classification: LCC PS8576.O724 A6 2021 | DDC C811/.54—dc23

Gordon Hill Press gratefully acknowledges the support of the Ontario Arts Council.

Gordon Hill Press respectfully acknowledges the ancestral homelands of the Attawandaron, Anishinaabe, Haudenosaunee, and Métis Peoples, and recognizes that we are situated on Treaty 3 territory, the traditional territory of Mississaugas of the Credit First Nation.

Gordon Hill Press also recognizes and supports the diverse persons who make up its community, regardless of race, age, culture, ability, ethnicity, nationality, gender identity and expression, sexual orientation, marital status, religious affiliation, and socioeconomic status.

Gordon Hill Press
130 Dublin Street North
Guelph, Ontario, Canada
N1H 4N4
www.gordonhillpress.com

CONTENTS

The Garden in the Midst

Los Angeles, 29 April – 5 May 1992

The poet's garden is the people.

Three Kings: 1992, 1968, 2020

The television played

the beating of a King

again and again,

never-ending beating just

to inform us now in 1992

twenty-four years after

the murder

of our great King:

now it's another–Rodney

King, construction worker,

poor, with his police record

put against him with the leather

and sticks of the police,

in the video of his arrest

a year ago. The strikes to his face are

brought back again, in-

forming us

over and over, the images,

replayed, remade

on television, now

that it was news again,

not fade away

history any longer,

now the police

had been set free again: the jury

in suburban Simi Valley

just

has found them not

guilty

of what we could see,

we had to see.

And Rodney stayed being beaten

on television

for being black

in black-and-white

video that clarifies his troubles:

being beaten

on television

for having little

but troubles.

That crime.

And Doctor King had been dispatched,
shot away, 1968, by the nation
of moon shots and citizen snipers. Shot
safely they thought
to eternity for the sin
of wishing them well.
So they were left
the unworthy, the failed
regents of justice here,
of that banished poetry.
Were you there when they crucified
my Lord? When they nailed him
to a tree?
Yes, you
were there. And now
again in 2020:

were you there when they crucified

George Floyd? You were there

when they nailed him

with a knee

into the concrete. Lord,

don't let it be

that your being

lynched on a tree

ever and again as on a loop

in hell, a video we repeat

of a being

beaten

O don't let it be

the image of what we are,

of what we always must

do. But establish

the justice, the poetry

that you were

and are to be,

the poetry that they

that we

kill you for.

The Garden in the Midst

Poetry, and the garden where it works
unwinding itself from the skein
of nothingness: poem and garden,
walled off, are pierced, penetrated,
and are helpless, open to everything
seen and unseen: the sawtooth
acetylene shriek of the airplane
passing over and soothed to a drone
by deep distance,
or the hush of tires from the far
highway, our surf here in the depths
of this continent of concrete:
auto-waves crumbling asphalt coasts
of the central sea: humans
who roll over one another, composing de-
composing ceaseless motion
that doesn't move

in the worldwide eye,

unblinking,

in the world's breast

that breathes as though asleep,

sleeping unbroken as though dead,

the world material

in which the human wave passes as a form

of torsion, of anxiety.

The wave

rises and is allayed

by its exhaustion, dying away

to rise again in the body

that merely lies, while poetry

and the garden in the midst

stretch out their roots and leaves:

their action is no stronger than a flower.

The Marigold

For instance, this marigold

        that stands, waking in the garden

and in the poem's regard, gathering

        and lacking power to refuse

everything that it needs.

        So it swallows the sun

and brings it here: the sun that in

a torture that never terminates,

or almost never, burns the elements,

so that sun fire

can linger in the marigold: the plant saves

the savage nobility of the one–

star and king–the eminence

without a body up there,

the sun, the light,

the one who is

only the bonfire of others.

The light of the sun, the light

that makes the sun, the one

without body up there, the one who is

only the burning of all others.

And the marigold also eats the smother
and rot within wet earth,
and brings them up here in its veins,
into the surface of flower: brings up
saps that flowed around broached caskets,
ichors that lay cooking on the inner melt
compressed by the weight
of everything that year by year
falls and is buried
by all that falls and is
buried later. Marigold
in the crannies of the bricks,
root in water and soil, face
in the sun's airy hands,
ruffled, bowed, beaten
by wind and rain, hail
and the early autumn snow,

unwinding yourself from the skein

beyond nothingness, most real.

There is no nothingness

beyond the mind,

no nothingness

but the nothing you ingest,

the nothing that comes to compose

the walls of your flesh,

composes your mouths and hands

that bring all things to your cells

where the anvil and hammer

and chemicals are busy

making it you.

The nothingness lay

in dark and was the dark

and then grew into you

and remains growing–it was never

nothing but always

the seed: the substance of last year's

vanished vanquished marigold.

The flower form and flesh I watch

unwaveringly, planted here

in the garden with you

is nothing, the gathering

of what you gather

in the shape given you

to take in passing: only

the form of your flight,

that kind of motion through the world

called "marigold":

a wave, a power, torsion

that swirls, forms and deforms

the elements, which it first created by its need

as it drives through them, needing

things to make up its body. Marigold,

gold that lives and laughs, gulping
the light in a long wilderness
more boisterous than soldiers
in the burning of a city,
more convivial than night's drunken pit,
freer than starved women freed from men
in the company of an adolescent god,
calmer, more silent than a saint's
contemplation from his hovel
in a steep forested gorge,
before him a river and cataract,
constellations of deer and wild sheep,
far behind him a white city.

The shining of gold, dark

        and blinding bright by turns,

the sun falling from blue clouds

        into the ocean and noon and dawn,

all unfolded and held up,

        carried, offered on motionless

petals, fingers, rays, unchanged

        through all the day's seasons

and the night under spectral

        low-watted garden bulbs.

Unchanged, marigold, except you always

are born, flower, last, and decay,

and mummified, brown and stiff, stand

in the snowy mud, shedding seeds.

Human Flower

Mary's gold, your flower primal

gold above and red gold underneath,

streaked with rust and blood,

earth ochre, stain of red clay,

knife wound, spike and spear thrust,

wrists tightly bound, thorns,

menses, a dripping scalpel line:

the seven sorrows, seven darts

that sum up all cuts

lopping the human parts away

perpetually: the darts that are your seeds,

that grow in, pierce, harrow,

fall from, and are, your heart.

Marigold, sun flower, sin flower,

like every flower

a body here

of the remote

star and fleshless dark,

the grasped grasping from here

of distant powers.

To be weary of time

is to be weary of oneself–

there is no time, only

your passing by and its form,

there is nothing but the inevitable

making

of what you choose: you have

no other body, nothing

but this making you

determined: potency that is perfect,

motionless, enchained, unfolding

death. And poetry and the garden

where it's made are nothing

but a flower in this sense:

each one is in the midst

of all others and is their form.

Los Angeles, 29 April – 5 May 1992

Los Angeles burns and this small back-garden

in Toronto is in its midst

burning blossoming, and is its form. The cries, shots,

crackling explosions of glass cracking

rise and spread from bodies surging

at the corner of Florence and Normandie

and all the corners of the starved

battered precincts, the poor

city in the great city, and they rise

from the impatiens in this garden's beds

exploding here, in its tangled mobbing green

and its flowers, red and orange, violet, rose

twisting with power as they grow asleep,

twisted by a light breeze in the shade

of the apple tree. The cries, shots, crackling

explosions of glass broken, like noises in a swound

or the last presence of the world when

vision sinks toward its consummation until

everything is swallowed

in pure dark, in pure light,

those two that are one: all things

revealed and ordered in calm glory

in the daylight, all things hidden

and growing asleep in the night,

the inner and perpetual

night in the heart

of earth, stone and hearth,

earth, blood and breath.

Suburban Simi Valley held the jury

that held the African was never beaten,

is not poor and has no reason.

That Oothoon was never raped,

does not sit lamenting on the shore.

And Ronald Reagan who was conjured

by the people, their effigy of fear,

of anger, of self

justification–Reagan who was pasted

with paper flowers and raised up, a venomous

float in a poor parade in the nice

parts of town while the living parts,

far over there, burned, and sent

their billows up

twenty-four years ago, in the terrible

night and bursting fires

of 1968, Reagan who was raised
as a shield when the African
cried and raged because the mothering
King was murdered...
Reagan while Los Angeles
burns again now hands
the Reagan Freedom Prize,
May 4, 1992 (look up,
can you see the smoke
in the sky over there?)
to Mikhail Gorbachev, the ceremony
being staged in Simi Valley.

Between the two acts in this valley,

verdict and award, falseness and self-praise:

sixty-three dead. And now rage gets tired,

a quiet gathers, brooms come out,

shards are swept, facades repainted,

and many words come out

to refuse, confuse the guilt

assigned by the African.

To the cry that he cried, O, there

is no deny! No possible denial.

But it is denied. By argument

that is a loud clapping of gums when the arguer

has no argument. Guilt was assigned

in justice and truth in South Central

and in Simi Valley not accepted: it was

the gods Palaver and Talking

Points who replied. So the hunger of

justice goes beggaring in the streets
again. An army, an ocean out of work,
a people, a world, bent to hate itself
and everything that is not itself
(and it refuses: you can hear
the torsion in its body
and soul as it refuses the hate forced in at it
and grows against hate to love: the dire
contest of the flower to blossom, life
in a scourged, surrounded body and soul).

A people bent first of all to hate

the poem. Because where the poor man

hungers and cries in the daylight where nothing

opens or in the night buys liquor

or drugs, a gun or a knife,

hustles in the street and runs

or creeps from flaming tattoos and frescoes

of the gang, and the grey and white

of the prowl car,

where the poor woman

lies down alone

in the wind through a cardboard

windowpane in the cold,

the roaches, the contempt

of children, in an eternal

remembrance in mind and muscle

of labor, inhuman, inescapable

for no reward, behind her and ahead:

her inheritance, her portion, her bread,

the place assigned–

the body given to her

and taken away, her way to be:

for there's nothing else allowed.

Where the poor woman and man

are married in the dearth

of goods, there is no garden

in the midst and no poem still

deeper in the midst, in the furthest

center of the garden

being made. Nothing is more foolish

in these concrete blocks and treeless streets

of bullets, squinting facades, rubble,

weeds, burnt frames, empty lots,

remorseless light through tall weeds, than talk

of the poem. There is nothing here except

the only wealth: the lives

of men and women as in fact

they are, not deformed and muffled up

by pastels, chromium, shaved

lawns, clipped hedges, electric

gates and topiary around

walled swimming pools, flowering trees,

gems fetched from a rape-pitted earth,

sculptures of chrome

in plazas behind fountains, muted abstracts

behind teak tables on sixtieth floors,

the cultivation of thoroughbreds,

big donations to the ballet.

Animated death.

Yet these, even these

simulacra

of life are also

fact alas, all human things

seem true, the passion of wealth

as much as any: to extract

more and more, to build out of pieces

of an earth rendered in pieces

a wall word-thick

and a bed soft, solid as surf,

as cloud, as bone-white

sand, as the last forest, the last

of the clear air: A bed all mine!

comes the scream of power

yearning for the restfulness its languid

fury angers for. (Yes, a bed wrenched

from a filthy mine, from blood

on the coal down underground.) A bed

all mine! A canopied bed

with butterscotch organdy as in ancien-

régime dreams to represent the sky,

a bed to rest in and not see, not dream

what it rests on. The cry dies away

and to our eyes, burning, comes

the sight not to be seen, even,

especially, in dream: the crush

of the Doric columns, the steel

pilings of the bed, and the airy bird-killing

plumes over Chernobyl and Bhopal,

the poison-fall

of the ruffled canopy to smother

the pike and the golden reed

in northern lakes. The whole mighty

creation of malevolent phantoms,

imperial energies in flight: these too

most real. Most real,

the despairing

gestures of denial from the rich

acidic mud: the stretching out,

the nearly emerging hand

of the damned

wealthy one

sunk in the slurry,

who took, fabricated,

profited, poisoned,

followed, served in a high

rewarded station

the soul of factory:

a single hand,

one finger managing

to escape a little, point to the sky

from the mud of his results

as it cools and hardens into rock,

into his destiny

of motionlessly scratching

inside the rock, motionlessly

wishing he could scratch.

No wealth can ever

be enough,

he thinks, racked fossil,

against the evergreen vision of poverty.

There must be more, a thicker wall,

a deeper bed, more distance, there must

be more. Must means desire,

and necessity, and rot. Must:

the word that has been made

such that we must live in it,

word that we are and shall be more

inescapably within, more even than now

we are within South Central
Los Angeles: burning there, and yet
in another place sparkling rich
in arrogance. More lost in must
than now we are lost in the virgin
forest we shaved away and left
bare, alone, a withered whore
now an inescapable
all-seasons labyrinth
of inferno
blistering all

around us. When the eternal
forests were ended and earth
turned to a wrinkled ball
falling through space, and the sunlight
shining through acid became
acid, an acid sea
began to drown and burn away
everything, even the walls
of human flesh. The humans–
those who were still humans then–loved
their scarred, crumbled city, and the sky,
the mighty wheel, stopped, and God,
they were told, was an official
of a star, well paid and publicized,
so they could look up to eminence
and say: we exist. And now this

is what the garden and the poem are

in the midst of, must

be in the midst of: these

are now the sky and earth we have,

the only one that roots

and petals have to draw through

and into themselves from farthest reaches

the beauty, substance, life,

the true living movement, to flower

here, in some form. Ravaged

woman, abraded man: you,

bent to despise the poem,

refused that bent. Utterly. Thanks. You are

the garden, and the only Eden,

in the midst of this. And you

are the small flower, marigold,

still deeper in the midst, the living

center, the poem making itself,

waiting in the travesty, the disaster

thrown on you, making it garden,

eating it, digesting it until

it flowers forth

longing and splendor,

paradise. Come see: rooted here

in my garden in Toronto, standing up

above the flowers is no

Greek or Roman garden god

in white-eyed blank-eyed

naked power and self-

deceptions of sexual

insouciance, of command by supernal

beauty, eternal stillness of the white

immobilized nude. The white god

is supplanted

by a bird feeder, a rough table,

a blank sheet and a written sheet,

two books, and my memory

of you, my hope of you:

these things are you

here with me now while still

we must remain apart.

Let no one lie: that the poem's nothing,

and nothing to you, and far away,

never known by you, entered

by you–that it brands

foreign names in white scars

on black continents

and stars. The poem

is in you who sing,

who most magnificently have

sung in disaster. It sings in you

its eternity, what flowers in blood and lights

in the eyes, what is made–in hands, on lips,

in the garden of all moments

of our lives: our hopes. As it is there

with you, so it is here: it's you

in the midst, whenever it's anyone

working among things, all

things, blossoms and concrete

and asphalt, it's you

working with remorseless

love bringing all that

to birth in you

so everything

may flower and sing.

Coda: The Zombies

No withered crone I saw
Before the world was made.
– Yeats

As the 1990s advanced

deeper into the white

tile floor and walls

and white lights burning

night and day of progress,

the zombies multiplied,

the living dead

not living really not moving

but moved around

on film and in the already infected

adolescence of video

and infancy of web pixels.

In Simi Valley and the nicer

parts of LA, they all watched, drunk

and stunned, the bloodless

dimmed tide mount around them

in poor color cinematography

shadows. An army of vivid darkness,

a night full of the not really

living dead remade

and remade again. A collector's

anniversary version provided

at decade's end for private purchase,

to replay the horror engulfing you

as often as you like, to party truly

like it's 1999. The pointed

and unwatched allegories,

just more crap after all,

of Bill Lustig: there they might have seen

Uncle Sam impaling people

with a flag pole in Twin Rivers,

they could watch the maniac cop

and would have been horrified

but never would think, not really, any more

than the dead really lived. They killed

but didn't live.

But what the tv watchers in LA
        and in Twin Rivers preferred,
to plain clear Uncle Sam
        and the cop, whether on the news
or in the gimcrack symbols of Bill Lustig,
        was the big-budget movie. They sleepwalked
to the phantasmatic boneyard, the netherworld,
        the afflicted ozone with ever-gaping-wider
holes in its flesh. They leaned, you could say
        were addicted, to the multifold
returns of the living though not living
        dead.
Though the watchers didn't really
        live either but still, talking
(really screaming) to themselves,
        they lived, sort of, in fear:

The zombies mean (they said, their lax

scared lips barely performing

a mouthing movement) my neighbors

in all the houses, cubicles, elevators,

sidewalks: stolid, dull, engulfing horde

coming toward me, jostling, stretching

to reach me, touch and if

a finger catches my finger

I'm one of them, thirsty

for blood because suddenly I know:

I don't have any. My whole day

and night is theirs now, staggering

to find a human–a boring plodding,

never resting, restless to absorb

another, another, not even

out of need. Maybe resentment.

And isn't my husband

one of them already? Why else

the dull talk, and the ugly

opinions not even spit out

with energy, just dripped

in a torpid frenzy

now and then, dropping

with a quiet wet thudding

like lame dragged footfalls on a filthy

bedroom floor or blood-slicked alley?

Haven't I already been touched

and more than touched, penetrated?

And isn't my son, then, dead,

though he moves, sort of,

in front of his screen? Or is he

behind the screen? And all of us

are behind the screen, flickers

in the night of the zombies,

and I'm infected, I'm half

dead and don't know. Except

sometimes I feel very dull and do know

that I've got no idea what they suffer,

those who suffer, far away, where they suffer,

unknown to me: the humans–

where they live, somewhere over there.

In poverty. Where is that?

We here waddle wealthy in the dark,

falling apart. I can't say I feel it except

something behind the eyes

seems to see without seeing.

How did I go in one instant from a girl

to a drooling withered

mind-gone crone, just able

to totter, just able

to see myself in a mirror,

a filthy yet reflecting

puddle, on a night of our crowd's

shuffling, the only sound

in deserted silence? And I see myself

and can't believe that this

is me

and I almost cry

but return

to my stumbling. But when

I did see myself back there,

O God, didn't I almost cry?

Coda: The Blues

The depression deepened, 1931,

and tanked the singing career

of Skip James: hard times

everywhere you go,

everywhere people drifting

door to door, dragging, slow,

nowhere a heaven-haven,

and who cares where they go?

The power, the drive, the engine

of that ancient lonesome song,

where did it come from?–

to light on those nine fiery

discs, eighteen songs set down

in Grafton Wisconsin for the self-named

paramount company. And Skip

did make with those discs

a celestial mode. And you know,

although you're turning

your back, you know

where the power came from

and where alone it comes from,

from what little tent

by what great river,

what onyx depth of indomitable

life, whose other lesser name

you hear sometimes

in your service: hope.

You know

what it sings:

        If just once more

ever I get up

        off of this killing floor

never again will I lie down,

        fall down, be pushed down here

or shot down, come back down–

        never anymore.

And Skip was silent then

        for thirty years: Nehemiah

James, waiting to come back jump

        back, skip the light

ecstatic, the troubled man,

        difficult often

to talk to, and build the walls again

in the growl and howl of his song

with their gates of plenty: fish gate, sheep gate

for all people. And magnificence,

their golden tower and their blast

furnace tower. To work again! To have

work! To walk at 7 a.m., the dew

on the little lawns of the houses

and concrete-curbed gardens of the projects,

thorn hedges with their waxen

orange and scarlet berries, to walk

swinging your dented, scratched

blue lunch bucket into U.S. Steel

over the Division Street bridge,

or to trudge the oak and elm guarded
side street, the trickle of your neighbors
tiding into another stream of workers
at every corner and finally
the spate on Main
where it flows north, and there you go by
the First and Last Chance: beyond it
you all pass in
to the Republic Works, its four stacks
sending their blue-grey drifts
out over poisoned scrub fields
of Joe Pye Weed in blue-grey flower
behind grey paintless houses. Even
that work, to have it and so dream

of other work. So not to be lying

in the streets in the idleness

of nothing anywhere near around

but shouts and shots, thinking nothing.

Bitterness. Except the voice even there

comes changing all to a bitter beauty

raising seeming corpses into determination,

into laughter. O Sam Hughes

with my father swinging

the heavy sledges in rhythm,

in my five-year-old eyes, breaking up

the dense concrete a dense

builder of houses had put there:

there in the dooryard where

the lilac grew. Breaking the concrete,

stubborn work–lavorare stanca–

and joyful, the barrier slowly

rendered to pieces, and there was room

for a flower bed now, a window,

and a door opening direct to my childhood

tree of the violet

essence of spring.

So thirty-three years later Skip came back, found again,

that was 1964, to build the gates

and walls anew. The attitude of him

cheered up slaves. His voice

building the city: the visible city

still very poor, but he builds the great

city in song, the women and men:

the crowds of them, their cry,

equality, diversity, that the soul

loves. Each one the sole love,

his or her precious open gait of a person
who never has stood in the presence
of superiors: for there are none.
Building the great city with hands
but first in the raging
sorrowing voice that ever
comes back. So tired, it cries, tired
of waiting for you, wanting alone
to love you: so tired
of groaning for you. And so glad,
so glad, it cries, yearning for you,
for you to love me (Come here!)
so glad that I don't know what to do.
Women and men alive

in the voice forever: just let it be.

            Let it get along. Can't we

all just get along? Let it sing? No matter

            what you do, it will,

will sing: I will

            love you. O promise me,

be just, be justice...

            just promise me

your love in return.

            Let this fire in me

not be smothered and scorned:

it cannot die but you can spill it

into the drains. But why?

And Skip James dead, the great King

sang the same–the final King for then,

until the new ones,

the old and young

throats of the dawn

song come round again:

Look, the sunrise–there God lives

and gives his light and heat away,

to birds, beasts, flowers and trees,

and there I take my lesson and say,

There is someone who loves you,
really loves you, has a life
for you that is life,
not a fabricated fever
of motion by imitation:
there is someone true
though you won't believe
who loves you:
guess who. You're turning
your back now
but you know who.

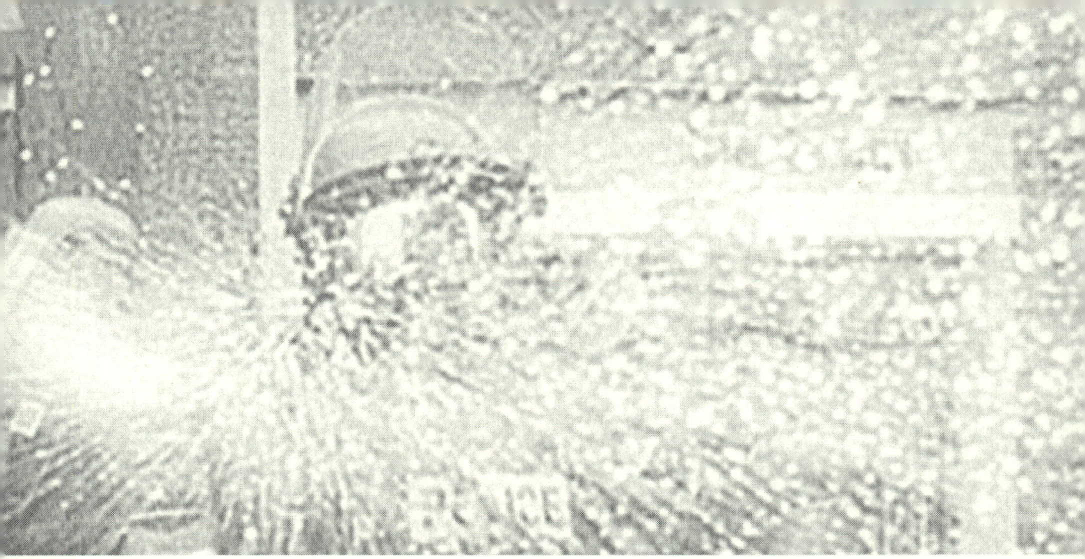

THE POET'S GARDEN

The poet's garden is the people.

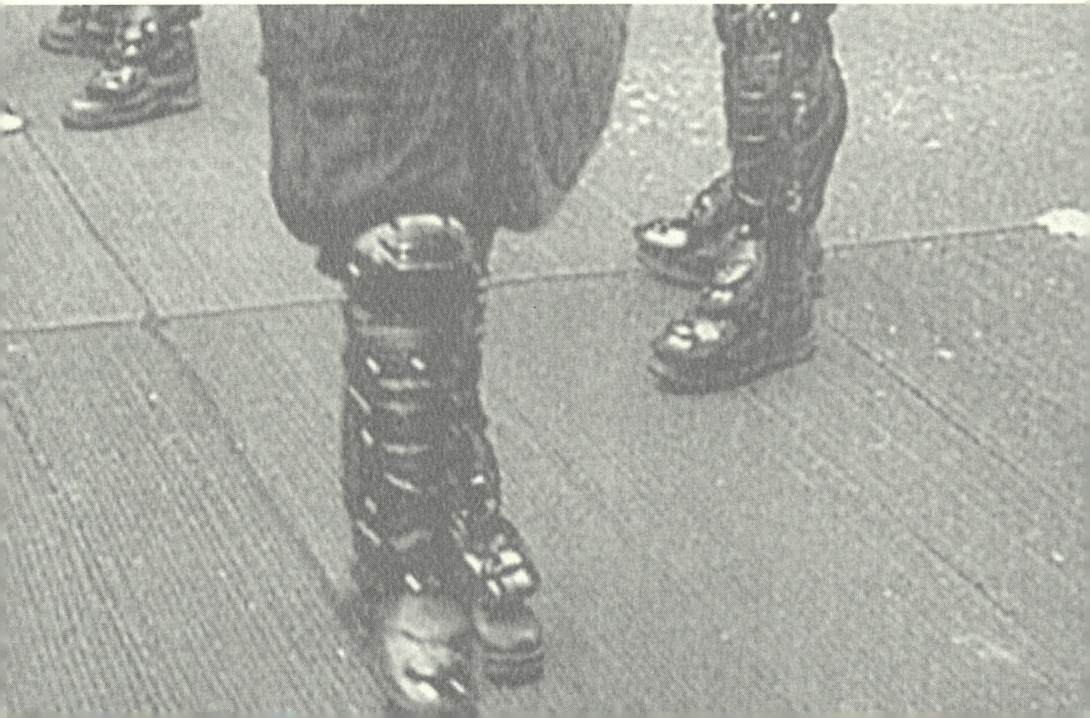

Garden and People

The Los Angeles riot of 29 April–5 May 1992 struck many with a sense that forebodings had come true. Similar though smaller outbreaks of violence, such as that in the Libertyville area of Miami in 1980, had foreshadowed it. The campaigns toward the November 1992 presidential election (Bill Clinton, President George H. W. Bush, Ross Perot) had also been touching on the suffering of the inner cities...gingerly. People were not in a mood to let the subject emerge into full consciousness, yet were aware that the inner cities' agony was only deepening despite the nation's wealth and its belief that it was humane, and competent to accomplish what it willed.

In the weeks preceding the riot, I'd been thinking about these things and their relation to my beloved vocation, poetry. The typical view would probably be that nothing could be further from this concrete, painful problem than a mandarin and disregarded art. But in fact there is an intimate and necessary linkage. I decided to write a poem on this subject. And just as I gathered my paper and pens and laid out everything on the round table in my back garden, to think and write in the early warmth of that spring, the riot began. A jury in suburban Simi Valley brought back a not-guilty verdict against the officers seen on videotape beating Rodney King, and the riot began.

Wide glass and screen sliding doors let my kitchen and its television communicate with the garden, so that as Los Angeles burned I simultaneously worked outside and followed the coverage. The television's murmur carried the news out into the lily-of-the-valley and lilac-scented air as I was trying to think and sing something that now came to include those events, to weave exactly contemporaneous occurrence into the earlier-planned work about their deep ever-present matrix. The very fact of the television news, but also its obvious inadequacies, its partialities and limitations of viewpoint, emphasized to me my own troubling co-presence with and separation from the unrest.

There in Los Angeles: rage, injustice piling up on injustice, more pain evolving out of pain. Here where I live: no choice for me, while hearing all this, but to know and worry about it from the midst of my own life, to live in my own rented house, to take care of and enjoy my garden. New bedding plants, blossoming, worked their way into the poem: impatiens for their name, marigolds for their association with the mother of mercy and their status in my thought as a sun-flower, hence a reminder of Blake's sunflower "yearning after that sweet golden clime", and of all Blake's human ideas and aspirations, his whole "prophecy against empire". Above me and in front of me: the great apple tree and the smaller crab apple tree were in brilliant white and rose blossom, and already the air began to fill with petals twinkling down to alight on my papers or in my coffee. There in Toronto I was perhaps as much in ancient China as in Los Angeles.

Someone with the luxury of sitting in his garden for seven days: is there sense in his thinking about poetry's isolation from the poor? And what poetry? What poetry is isolated from the poor? Isn't it only the poetry of the rich? Or rather, of the "middle sort", the clerkly class, which serves the rich, and which is tempted to arrogate to its own sort of poetry the sole title of Poetry? For the poor have their own poetry. At the time I was well up on the debate among various rappers and rap groups–it had reached a high pitch just a few weeks before the riot–over which ones could validly claim the authenticity of the streets. Which had really come from the mean neighborhoods? Which could claim to know with living knowledge, with experience, what the song-poems talked about?

"The poor and low have their way of expressing the last facts of philosophy as well as you", said Emerson, using "as well as" in a way that almost certainly influenced Whitman's "every atom belonging to me as good belongs to you". Emerson showed that the poet is the "representative person" because expression is the poet's whole calling and all things are essentially expression. But can we condemn, as too far from living expression, the poet of what we often mean by "poetry"–the poems in widely known magazines, in big anthologies, in books from New York and London publishers and prestigious literary and university presses? For certain, what goes by the name of poetry includes items governed by the human intellect's flaw of a drift away from reality, or a flight from it, or even the self-deception of a proclaimed "approach to reality" that is in fact all theory. But this is never true of real poetry, great poetry.

The poet's garden is the place where the somatic experiences of childhood, which maturity and responsibility leave disastrously behind, are ever renewed. Those thousands of encounters with ants and beetles, the cutting sharpness of pine needles and blackberry thorns and leaf edges, the smells of earth, grass, plants, rot and dung, sap and mildew and blood, the million textures of light on every sort of thing, the cavortings of cats, squirrels, jays and robins. Every day the poet is in the garden and experiences–which is to say, enjoys–all the substance and pattern from which is made our basic knowledge of being on the earth. Those are the experiences which, gathered in early childhood days, are known from then on as an inner garden. Known this way even in hard human lives, whose childhood world is utterly different from the one I've described, more a matter of bricks and waste lots, wet dark alleys, boarded-up houses, railroad lines a few feet behind the dining room and bedroom. Primordial reality, known just so, always in a unique form, in every human life except perhaps those destroyed at the very root by absolute disaster and cruelty.

But most people become "doers"–mature and responsible–and doers leave the garden, whether they choose to or are forced. Then the garden, relegated to childhood, now a memory, submerged into the inmost levels of body and mind–the garden becomes only an unconscious base of action in a world that is utterly divorced: the serious and public place of the fight to gain eminence, or safety, or at least "enough". The doers have correctly interpreted a poetic allegory of the garden, a lesson of which childhood seemed little aware. The battles of sparrows over seeds, the twisting of branches to get out of each other's shade and find the light and so not be starved to death, are known by doers for what they are. The garden may appear a place of rest, harmony, and pleasure, but it also means something else. No matter how it is regulated toward peace by the aspiring hands of human beings, of gardeners, it remains a site of life's mortal struggle: "And the whole little wood where I sit is a world of plunder and prey."

The doers see this. And the brutal lesson of competition is practiced–out of the sheer impossibility of escaping it. Sometimes it's practised with resolution or even with joyful abandon, sometimes in sheer hopeless weariness or terror. As for the garden itself, it waits behind the house, empty all day and all night, weeklong, because to the people who own the garden it is largely a flickering dream. They are out fighting for a living, and if they don't succeed, they think, the garden could not exist. So it remains there, rarely entered, a permanent possibility used as a brief, occasional retreat.

But the poet's garden is first of all the people, and the people are first of all the excluded and poor. The garden can also be in the enclosed greenery, but it is first of all in the street. It can be in the facts of sap and chitin, but it is first of all in the human facts.

Poet and Street

Immediately after the uprising, an edition of ABC News's *Nightline* program originated from South Central Los Angeles: May 4, 1992. At the neighborhood meeting that ABC had organized in the hall of a local church, one of the speakers was a poet: a street poet, an oral poet. Not a rapper exactly, but a chanter, who, though clearly influenced by rap, was part of a tradition that in its present form must go back in the United States hundreds of years. This tradition is part of what in fact led to rap, according to many artists–Bo Diddley was one example–who have spoken of street chanting as prominent in their own childhoods and as a basis of their lyrics and music.

Such poetry includes elements of folk ballad and traditional newspaper verse. And these two traditions, prior to newspapers and down to our own day, came together in ballads and chants that told the stories of recent events and made them poetry. Almost everyone can think of "Frankie and Johnny", "Stack-o-Lee" ("Staggerlee"), "The Wreck of the Old 97", "The Wreck of the Edmund Fitzgerald", "Springhill Mining Disaster", "The Lonesome Death of Hattie Carrol", and so forth. Long ago such ballads were printed in "chapbooks" (cheap books) or on sheets, "broadsides", and sung by the tramping singers, so the songs of famous events could be heard. Then the sheets were sold for singing by locals once the chapman was gone. The traditions of the folk ballad and the broadside ballad, whether in England or elsewhere (e.g., Appalachia, the Smoky Mountains, Newfoundland), often produced poems with the combined functions of bringing the news, fixing and memorializing it, even making it legend, and often combining it with some explanatory, community-affirming sentiment or value, some universalizing moral significance.

The Los Angeles street poet's chant sang brilliantly and clearly, like a spate of fresh spring water, compared to the American language that most *Nightline* viewers were solely accustomed to: technical and bureaucratic language and middle-of-the-road conversation. Did it simultaneously affront them and seem sub-literary, accustomed as they were to dealing with literature (if at all) through written texts? But it was striking and important precisely in being typical of all experiences of real (unrecorded) performances. In this respect it was especially important to be loved and pondered–though it probably was not received as such–by average contemporary Americans: television watchers. Suddenly reality sang out, beyond even the forceful statements of opinion from the other speakers: reality in terms of the perfect fusion of voice, passion, experience, response, thought–a meaning more comprehensive yet simpler than "meaning" in our usual sense. And upon its conclusion, of course, the whole work of art began fading into memory as it had already faded into silence. The television had brought a glimpse of the oral poet, working by memory and chant, generally in the streets, performing his art and sending it off into the air, and into the heart and mind of the alert and the generous, without books or any other recording technology.

He was almost certainly unknown to much of the literary world, perhaps little known to the world beyond those who could meet and hear him. He was almost entirely without a national readership, without permanence for his songs in most libraries, perhaps without recognition beyond his community. "Leaving great verse unto a little clan" is how Keats characterized this type of poetry. In the *Nightline* program he is not identified. The moderator gives him the floor–"The brother, over there"–and the crowd in the meeting room of the First A.M.E. Church, stirring because of previous speakers, is shushed–"Shhhh! Quiet!"–and then the poet steps forward from a standing portion of the crowd of about 150 and recites.

He's young, mid-twenties, with a contained pulsation of energy. Lean and tall, dreadlocks swept to the back and falling down along his neck and the back of his head, strong narrow jaw, planar cheeks, well-shaped mustache coming down a little past the corners of the mouth, small chin beard, one earring on a short chain from the left ear–a flickering flat metal symbol of a half moon. Wearing a black bucket hat with the Malcolm X "X" in silver on its front. He doesn't have the weight of a "leader" but the rapier-like aspect of the leader's chief hero.

He delivers with perfect enunciation of crisp consonants, resonant vowels, in a clipped, dynamic, rapid but not too rapid rhythm between speech and chant. Taking the floor quickly, he gives a brief introduction to what he's about to do and to the subject of the town hall meeting: *I don't have a question. You ask why this is happening. Cuz...*

My-Country-'Tis-of-Thee
Is a racist land of liberty
Land where my father died
Cuz he was chained and he was tied
From every mountainside
And justice rings...

No justice no peace
First there was quiet
Then there was a riot

This was a dedication to Rodney King
Who was ridin' down the road–
Nine out of ten, didn't do a thing
Just the color of his skin
Was enough to bring him in
Dead or alive
Lucky to survive

We all saw it on the news show
L A P D Ge – sta – po
And thanks to the video
That was shown and shown
We all know
What black folks have always known:

Out in the streets
Don't worry 'bout the thief
You better worry 'bout the po – lice chief

We'd rather have the in – mates
Than have Daryl Gates
And be living in the po – lice state

No justice no peace
First there was quiet
Then there was a riot

During his recital, a girl can be seen in the background, at the front edge of a standing part of the crowd, wearing a white t-shirt with elbow-length sleeves, her arms folded across her waist. At the end, the camera catches him stepping back to her–much shorter than he is, wearing a small smile–and taking her hand–their hands search for and find each other and close–which further brightens her still restrained grin. They both quickly turn back to paying attention to the front of the room, which echoed now with the aftermath of his song.

Alas, the poet is never identified by name, as is the case with most of the other speakers too. I've searched and searched for him, for his identity, and still hope someday to find it. The transcription is my own, made from a recording of the *Nightline* program, and I want to make a few comments on it. Like so many ballads and popular poems, the poem used "wrenched accent", which isn't reflected in the transcription: thus, "Liberty" was pronounced "Li – ber – TEE", to slow the word and emphasize the rhyme. A crucial instance was the word "Gestapo": "GEH – STAH – PO", with the long o of the final syllable drawn out and emphasized even beyond the first two. This introduced the o sound as a powerful unifier, and the poet strongly linked the sound to "police", using an effect like wrenched accent to bring out the frequent African American pronunciation of "police" as accented on the first syllable with a long o. So "POE – LEECE – STATE" later in the stanza "rhymed" with "GES – TAH – PO." Another thing that was hard to convey in the transcript was the brilliant use of the last line, or half line, of the first stanza, "and freedom-rings", or "and freedom rings". The phrase was constructed with bitter irony to mean the metal rings that a slave might be chained to–'freedom' rings–and at the same time to introduce the refrain–i.e., "And Freedom rings: 'No justice, no peace...'"

What was essential about South Central Los Angeles at that moment was materialized by this poet. He had taken the floor towards the end: at the fifty-minute mark of the hour-long program. His neighbors participating in the program had listened with demonstrative approval.

Poem and poet were a sort of summation, an effect perhaps strengthened, who knows, by ABC's editing. In any case, for the news program the poem fulfilled the summative role magnificently. In its grasp and fusion of all the elements properly belonging to it, it had a precision and lucidity almost never seen on television. The chant was in part a dark report on disaster, in part a cry of pain, in part a sign of consolation and encouragement in the face of injury, in part a howl of bewilderment, and in part an expression of creative joy, hope, and unremitting courage, in part a demand for plain justice, in part a call to arms and at the same time a call for fellow-feeling from the surrounding society.

The poem had given the essential. What was the essence of the local people`s participation in the television meeting? "Confusion" is one answer that the hostile or the puzzled might want to give. As Ted Koppel, the moderator of *Nightline*, brought out during the program, many of the participants' interpretations of the riot, and often their suggested solutions and demands, were inconsistent, mutually exclusive, contradictory. And the same point has often been used, of course, to criticize many of the African-American responses to the riot offered in the following months. And it is often used to criticize the voices of almost every liberation movement.

It's a vapid, false criticism. Contradictions among the responses do not make them invalid. In these apparent contradictions there is a profound, realistic encounter with a multifold problem. There is a profound, realistic unity of aspiration and despair, and of goodwill and contempt, of admiration and hatred, towards the tormentors of the poor, towards the surrounding, down-pressing society. In logic, such disparate and antagonistic elements cannot be maintained together. The surrounding culture prefers paper logic. Falsely identified with "reason" and "intelligence", this method brackets out any whole look at the fact supposedly under consideration. But humanly, all the elements in the so-called contradictions found under oppression are the aspects of a unity. The supposed contradictions expressed on *Nightlin*e showed the living fact of South Central Los Angeles in 1992: a community forced to suffer as both victim and subordinate replicator of its own outsider-imposed pain, and then made to suffer again when criticized for its division over "solutions".

Let's take examples of these contradictions. If one African American says his people have to stand on their own, and the "conservatives" in the surrounding society applaud, while another African American says that his people must receive some aid and compensation for what has been denied them and imposed on them, and must receive a truly fair and a much more effective enforcement of legal justice, and the "liberals" agree, is this a contradiction? In fact, both resolutions are completely, simultaneously true.

This contradiction is itself an expression of what tortures them, what birthed them and partly formed their identity. Living this contradiction is, for now, their only way to exist in a two-faced nation. One needs must love one's origin, one's childhood, one's native place, however awful; one must love it at least a little, or die. This "contradiction" is a truth that must be manifested and must be listened to, respected, and acted upon. But in a world that disregards poetry and prefers ersatz logic, it can only appear as a contradiction. The dominating group's only real effort expended on the so-called contradiction will be an effort to eliminate it: to eliminate the truth.

Some riot victims voiced a contemptuous dismissal of all trust in anything beyond their own community. Others took the opposite stance, addressing the larger American community almost exclusively, demanding that it provide justice and compensation. Nothing less than maintaining, poetically, both of these "mutually exclusive" positions can get at the full and real situation. Justice is something that must be given the oppressed because as a matter of power it can't be obtained by them solely through their own efforts. On the other hand, there is not the slightest historical evidence, or logical demonstration, that justice ever will be rendered to the oppressed, in view of motives in the social structures that built the justice system.

This situation necessarily moves the oppressed to attempt some sort of compensatory self-reliance that will be fully satisfactory in itself. The shortfalls of this effort, given the unfair allocation of opportunity and resources, necessarily provokes occasional outbursts of frustration.

This in turn is used to cover up a beautiful fact: it is the poor, such as the riot victims and even the rioters in South Central Los Angeles, who are our Founding Fathers and Founding Mothers of today. For the Founders have not died out. It is the poor who continue that unfinished revolution. The poor, and they alone, understand the promise of the founding ideals and documents. They alone push for the full, real implementation of what the word and idea "America" means.

The analysis of the supposed contradictions could be continued through every one of them. But still this would leave us far short, with nothing on our hands but a list of statements. But the street poet's chant gathered all the contradictions into a single living form. On the level of proposition and logical cohesion, it must have seemed lacking to many *Nightline* viewers. And yet, I believe that anyone who saw his performance and thought back on it honestly would realize, and admit, that its significance, though extremely complex, was precise and perfectly clear. That significance was the totality of the South Central Los Angelans' knowledge of and reaction to reality, which no proposition can reach.

In our day, technology, science, rationalized discourse of all types, and mass communications have minimized–often actively intending and seeking to do so–the relevance and credibility of poetry. The street poet's poem makes us see that we will never understand the people who provoked the riot, police and jurors and their encouragers, and we will never understand the people who participated in it and suffered from it, the inhabitants of South Central Los Angeles, unless we to listen to them in a certain way, a poetic way: attention to the whole reality. But this truth is occluded by police barricades, gated communities, segregated zip codes, massive imbalance of wealth and power. It can come only from an attention to and grasp of the whole that is beyond all possible analysis, all technology, science, logical discourse of any type, and mass communications. These things can at best be aids to and tools of poetry. The street poet's poem was simply participating in the nature of poetry. Its nature is always to involve life's contradictions and the way they are necessary to one another, but are surpassed in a mutual unity that comes partly from the pure act of living and partly from the intentional exercise of artistic creativity.

Those who today happily and even proudly ignore poetry ignore the place where they would meet the full complexity and completeness of human being. What they are ignoring is the richness of life. They are self-protectively ignoring, also, the pain of realizing that their disasters come largely from the fact that life does not open to the methods they have committed themselves to–let's say it more bluntly: limited themselves to. Of course, the fullness of life belongs first of all to life itself, and all the scorners of poetry naturally pat themselves on the back, if they ever think of the issue, for being human, for having a soul just as well as the next guy. In other words, they think that they inherently have sufficient poetry. Well, the human being also inherently has chemistry. That does not mean that one can know anything about it and do much with it without chemists and the whole science of chemistry. In the same way, we delude ourselves if we think we have any access to our soul, and any chance and means to develop our soul–any chance or means to be human–without poetry.

Analysis–the Poverty of Power

Every analysis will fail that begins–as any analysis must–with its choice of one pole of a dichotomy, for instance that aid must be given from without or that responsibility must be demanded from within. Even the awareness we now begin to find in public policy that these two positions must be blended is only a partial and belated recovery, through the experience of repeated policy failures, of a fact that the poem offers whole and that poems have always offered whole. Further, even this growing awareness in its rationalized form of policy construction is inadequate, since it includes the wrong and impossible necessity that the riot victim be separated from the riot perpetrator. As poetry knows, these two are often one. In a deeper sense, in fact, they are always identical: a community will not produce riots unless its citizens are conscious of their status as victims. A poetic vision–a comprehensive and whole vision–always knows this, and it is sometimes affirmed, though then it is quickly submerged by a flood of the analytical, partial approaches we prefer–are addicted to. For instance, there's the statement about the August 1965 Watts Rebellion that Bayard Rustin made in *Commentary* a few months after the events: "The whole point of the outbreak in Watts was that it...was carried on with the express purpose of asserting that they would no longer quietly submit to the deprivation of slum life." Despite important shortcomings, Rustin's essay proclaimed the fact that the Watts rebellion had a purpose and expressed it. But even as this fact was voiced by fair and alert observers, it had already been rendered inaudible by the fury of disagreement over whether the riot had been a pure demand for justice or a mere violation of law and order, and other such univocal and hopelessly inadequate approaches based on creating dichotomies.

The street poet's poem and his community's love of it reveal that the South Central Los Angelans knew how they had been placed in a situation designed to instill self-loathing by means of deprivations, pressures, and assaults, and thus an externally imposed self-image. This knowledge in itself was resistance, a refusal of these impositions. They had been placed in a situation in which self-reliance and external aid (or simply fair treatment from others) are equally necessary and yet are re-engineered by the dominant society so as to seem to interfere with each other. This terrible dilemma was thrust into their life. Their oppression could not be solved entirely from within, but solved from without as alms, as someone else's gift, it would not be solved at all. Somehow, the without and the within would have to be blended, just as they are in life and poetry, and just as they are not in our basic way of thinking, analytical, power- and efficiency-directed.

Can we disentangle ourselves from this mess we have made? Is it more than a mess? And are we really trying? For it turns out to be convenient for the chief perpetrators and benefactors of inequality that the almost universally imposed analytical rather than poetic approach to reality creates a sense that the problem is inevitable. This seems to remove guilt from the powerful strata of society, and even from most citizens. It removes the stimuli of personal guilt and the energy born of faith that a solution is possible. From this follows the bitter "whatever" that quickly becomes the return to the board room.

But the African American community itself is always keeping in mind that solutions are not simple, but this does not mean that they are not possible. It is the nation as a whole that has created its painful paradoxes. It is the nation as a whole which has the absolute responsibility to provide effective, definitive aid. It is clear that, to put it simply, the answer to organised greed and theft is the people through the government enforcing equable sharing via taxation and social spending. This the African American community remembers and calls for, and justice and social improvement demand that the down-pressing society must let up its pressure and at least accept the hand the African American offers. Instead, it continuously demands self-reliance from the oppressed, ignores the impressive self-reliance that actually exists, and gestures toward a self-arrogated responsibility for its failed attempts at redress.

Not long before his assassination, Dr. King dealt with the manufactured contradiction of continuing to deprive the oppressed of adequate resources while preaching self-reliance to them–what he termed "the boot-strap philosophy". In fact, self-reliance and social aid are a unity, he said in his speech "The Other America", in the version given at Grosse Pointe, Michigan on 14 March 1968. "Now certainly it's very important for people to engage in self-help programs and do all they can to lift themselves by their own bootstraps.... I think there is a great deal that the black people of this country must do for themselves and that nobody else can do for them..." And then he added the necessary contradiction: "to have freed the negro from slavery without doing anything to get him started in life on a sound economic footing, it was almost like freeing a man who had been in prison many years and you had discovered that he was...innocent of the crime for which he was convicted and you go up to him and say now you're free, but you don't give him any bus fare to get to town or you don't give him any money to buy some clothes to put on his back or to get started in life again."

The frustrations induced by contradictions among the self-styled custodians of society give rise to a common reaction among them, namely, avoidance: the attempt to assert that such expressions as the South Central Los Angeles riot are not worthy of response aside from increased police repression. Even while the riot was under way, many "conservatives" were trying to deny that it was spontaneous and meaningful. Some South Central Los Angelans, they claimed, merely feigned a rage that fuelled a false revolt. This argument contended that South Central Los Angeles was burnt largely by fires set on purpose by people who had no passion of freedom but took an opportunity for their own profit and pleasure: a festival of chaos in which tastes could be indulged and goods carried off. Such purpose, even in a few, is supposed to show a lack of sincerity that disqualifies the uprising from receiving a hearing as expression: it can only deserve honor if it is a purely reflexive cry of agony. To treat the riot as a cry, said the conservatives, would be to reward criminals.

But this attempt to delete the riot's significance is useless, since even the most calculating criminal cannot avoid being an expression of his milieu. Such violence as that of the riot, even if every individual act within it were crass and purposive, could not occur without a context of despair. Without a pre-existing environment of horror, even a rebellion would not take place because there would not exist a sufficient number of persons moved to the necessary bitter calculation. No outburst of many ordinary men and women, within which the criminals could hide, would occur. No "critical mass" could be achieved.

During and after the riot, voices were raised, on behalf of the rioters and in some cases from some of them, which explicitly championed riot as resistance. I am going further. The riot, even in its criminal acts, and even if every single act composing it turned out to be criminal, would still be a true and necessary expression of injustice and the demand for justice. Its violence is first of all and primarily the violence of the repression that provoked it and created the conditions for it. Put the blame there–not "also" there, but there first and foremost. Put the punishment there. To preserve law and order, send the police and the military there. The riot raised the question of the legitimacy of the order achieved in the enforcement of the present laws. Of course, "legitimacy" means "actions or states of society in conformance with the law". Thus the riot also raised the question of the legitimacy of the present legal system itself.

And there is, of course, no doubt at all that this riot was far from being totally, or even in an important measure, calculating and inauthentic. Nevertheless, the conservative element in the nation kept insisting that the issue was hoodlumism versus law and order. This "conservative" riposte, even if true, would be empty. But it was false. And it is crucial, too, to keep in mind that riots usually occur because the police–supposed guardians of civil order–act criminally, thus suspending the community consent to be policed. This was the case not only with the 1992 South Central Los Angeles uprising; it had already been the case with the beating of Rodney King a year earlier, and it was the case with the judicial exculpation of the offending officers that sparked the uprising. In justice and truth, the conservatives' cry against the riot on behalf of "law and order" would have had to be aimed first against the police and courts. Those were the institutions that first, most massively, and provocatively, broached law and order.

Similarly, the elements of criminal violence in the riot resembled and were connected to familiar ideas by which the wealthy and powerful have established their theoretical foundations. The basic principle of modern utilitarianism is that growing wealth is what enhances the lives and rights of all citizens, and that wealth in turn only grows by separated and selfishly motivated acts of individual persons and entities striving for profit, power, security and eminence. The selfishly motivated violence of an individual criminal within the riot serves the self-expression of the poor on exactly this same principle. If the profit-taking of the average citizen or corporation, which is often ruthless and which is specifically encouraged to be so, contributes to the prosperity and growth of his society, then it has to be admitted, at a minimum, that a widespread outbreak of get-it-while-you-can chaos will arise in a social sector where no worthwhile profit, security or eminence is available. There, an outbreak like the 1992 uprising is often the best simulacrum of the dominant society's philosophy and behavior that the oppressed have.

If we want to discriminate among fires, and say that in the riot there was a false fire and a true, or even that it was all false, then we're saying simultaneously that in our whole society the case is the same. The United States too burns with a calculated flame, much of it false and destructive, using and eating and reducing to ash whatever it decides to take.

Death-in-Life

The United States is a disheartened country. It is not mainly out of inhumanity that this society as a whole and the powerful sectors within it omit to do anything effective for the disadvantaged–especially for those groups, such as the African Americans and the Native Americans, perennially disadvantaged in a way that belongs to the origins and essence of the nation. The absence of commitment to real change is an intentional position that buttresses the current imbalance of opportunity and resources. The resulting national impasse, which no individual or group can break, fosters in the dominating group a resentful self-defensiveness: "It's not my fault, I don't want things to be this way, but I was not here when they were formed, and I have proved to myself that I can't affect them, so don't put it on me, leave me alone, if there's a solution it has to come from somewhere else."

Until we believe in equality, nothing will change. And there will be no such belief until we dispel the rhetoric that creates privilege-based metaphors that presume that action occurs from "outside" or "above". This rhetoric retains power exactly where it already is. Instead, action must come through total social acceptance and cooperation, based on an idea of society that grows ever more open.

Until such action arises, most Americans in the well-off portions of society will continue to behave, as now, like the sailors in Samuel Taylor Coleridge's "The Rime of the Ancient Mariner". Once long ago the sailors thoughtlessly applauded the Ancient Mariner's thoughtless killing of a bird, and so they "owned" the murder. Now a supernatural being has taken retribution against them for their crime. They have died and have been reanimated so that, turned into mere automatons, they can sail the ship that bears the Mariner himself, the only remaining living soul. He still lives because he was the one man aboard who had at least the courage to act, and afterwards the courage to accept his guilt and its consequences: his new destiny. Like those sailors, we have denied that the crime is ours, but we participated in it by benefitting from its results and refusing to relinquish the benefits and not admitting they were criminal. Or trying to forget it. As a result, we are not permitted a destiny of our own, and we are not permitted to accomplish the intentions that we self-pityingly claim as virtuous, as proving our virtue. We are the living dead.

Coleridge's sailors are an important image for us to contemplate because, both before and after their deaths, they are animated. Dead, they still work their ship with precision and success. But back when they first set sail, and they were still really alive, their technical skill had served a mercantile purpose, and the ship was likely to return home, bring wealth, and sail again. After their crime and their death and re-animation, the voyage was utterly changed. Their work as automatons would get the ship back to home port, but only for one last time. At the very moment of delivering the Ancient Mariner to the shore and to the completion of his destiny, his truly living destiny of atonement, the ship sank and the sailors fell down: their use was over and they became mere corpses. Which was *their* destiny.

Coleridge realized that what is vital cannot be distinguished from what is stultifying and deathly simply according to the categories of the active and the still. The sailors, who had forfeited their souls through cowardice and conformity and denial of responsibility, worked furiously although in fact they were now dead. The poet knew that there is a real but false, ultimately destructive energy, which he called "death-in-life". This is a man-made imitation of life intended to avoid life and its problems, especially the problem of death. By this death-in-life, human beings divert their own energies to the purpose of shielding themselves from real life and real death, from the true fact of the human situation. This death-in-life has its own energy: restrictive regulation explodes and grows over everything, injustice spreads with determination, dullness seeks relentlessly to impose itself everywhere, meretriciousness burns more and more of the earth for fuel and builds itself bigger monuments of the dead.

In the United States in the 1990s, the well-off knew they were possessed by a manic and apparently creative energy: signs of prosperity and triumph abounded. The trick is the right interpretation of the signs. Hart Crane saw–and tried to read a humane prophecy of renewal into–the immense activity of skyscrapers, mills, cars, roads, dams, bridges. And how much more had been added since his day! The desire for more–more rooms, more lawn, more paintings, more horses, more walls, more seclusion, more eminence, more control over others, more freedom from what one's own rapaciousness reduces those others to and from the stink and poison it creates–drives an endless proliferation of techniques, goods, secured enclaves, modes of exclusivity and of triumph over rivals, ever-shifting trends in the fashions of greed and elusive satisfaction.

Not everything that looks like a flowering is equal. It's possible to separate the lively and creative from the furious mechanism of simulation and ever-intensifying routine. There is a real power. Mental power, Wordsworth called it: it often acts, yes, but it is also identical with stillness, with receptivity, with self-forgetful contemplation of other beings and quiet fellowship with them. It was necessary, Wordsworth said, to be *both* "a sensitive / And a creative soul". To be a soul at all, there must be the hard creative work of receiving and giving, and of giving as a result of, and from the enrichment of, what has been received. There must be a "wise passiveness", to use Wordsworth's words again. Creativity comes forth from receptivity. Activity comes forth from passivity–or better to say from acceptance, since this pole of our being is also deeply *active*–requires inner, creative *action.*

But in addition to this power, the only true power, the only thing worthy of the word "power", there is a horrible parody of it: a physically in-motion but deeply immobile spectacle, a self-seeking yet self-destroying rigidity. There is this parody, this travesty of true power, which masquerades in a willed, pointless, delusory frenzy, a furious but static motion feverishly, mistakenly claiming to be capacity and action. This motion is the rhythm of our cities where they are successful in their own official terms: the rhythm of traffic, of subterranean machinery, of industrial air conditioning, of the gaseous and liquid billows of pollution, of the tides of sewage, of binary switching.

But where our cities are perpetually unsuccessful by their official standards, in their slum housing and rows of boarded up storefronts and expanses of vacant lots, the rhythm is quite different. It's a calmer rhythm in these places where relatively few inhabitants are required to be anywhere, or even wanted anywhere. There's little that would make them leave in the morning and come back around five...except for those of course who can be maids, cleaners, nannies... A rhythm prevails that is calmer, but more intense and deep. A pulse. An actual pulse. It's a rhythm often crossed by seemingly random unrhythmic elements, gentle or violent: the idle isolation of the fearful in apartments, the drifting of the unemployed at corners and in bars, angry shouting, shots, the scream, the siren, arguments breaking out, or laughter breaking out, at corners or in alleys or at bars and barbeque places; perhaps music above all, all the poetry flowering from the Blues. That "one bad stud" who "don't wear no hat and Lord he don't wear no shoes / He just hangs on the corner singing old country blues"...by poetically dwelling in a new Jerusalem, he can survive and even rejoice while shoeless in Babylon the Great. And in his lyrical exultation, he can include the full horrible reality of the present. The downtown glass and chrome rhythm expresses energies diverted from life. This other rhythm expresses our urban life as it is at the living root: the "green vine angering for life", as Wallace Stevens put it.

Not often enough listened to, the counterpoint of these rhythms was made forceful by the performance of the street poet, his jagged complex original rhythms, exaggerating his chant and his accent, the propositional emptiness of his poem, its fullness of vision, on ABC television. How homeless the poet was, how essentially "at cross purposes", in the arithmetical grid of the broadcast's information segments between carefully timed commercials, in its intransigent demand that all who appear on it, though forced to truncate their thought and feeling by restrictions of brevity and discontinuity, must nevertheless present themselves as reasonable, coherent, measured, modest, polite, and succinct. Above all, succinct. The show must be kept moving along. Anything too lengthy is boring television. Precisely because the poem had none of these characteristics, it had content and was truly expressive. It contradicted the television program's demand for the empty but exact miming of reasonableness. This was one obvious-to-everyone meaning that it had, obvious even to those who would say they couldn't understand it. It contradicted the requirement for familiar, useless, repetitive styles of thought and presentation–and so it was original and authentic. It expressed what is known and felt in its own time and place by people who are eminently alive to their crisis.

From Rigidity to Reason

Much of America's success, due to its lack of authenticity, has acquired the rigor of a willed and willful frenzy. What we do is repetitive. We study methods of creating power and wealth, we formularize them, we repeat them, we train ourselves and our children to be just what they require, we demand of anyone who wishes to approach us that he or she be recognizable by the formulae. Our wish, of course, is that the ever more desperate furor with which we do all this should somehow turn into an expression of a true energy, of a drive for a "better life" in some reasonably noble definition of the term. But we only succeed in cannibalizing energy to produce an always falser and more congealed simulacrum. Our terms for these linked operations are "exploitation of natural resources" and "manufacture".

What characterizes us is repetitiveness–a repetitiveness that we fatally disguise to ourselves as its opposite, change. We are constantly telling ourselves that this is the era of change and unprecedented inventiveness. We love to repeat that more innovation has occurred in the last few years than in all the preceding centuries, that the electronic communication age we are forever pushing further is a transformation as profound as the industrial revolution or the development of agriculture and cities. Nothing could be less true.

The change we're addicted to, change of a technical kind, is the form that empty repetition and conformity have taken in our time. Nothing a person can pursue today can render him or her less original, more inauthentic, more a mere follower of the unexamined habit of everyone, than change in the sense of technical innovation and of applying new techniques to produce more wealth, power, efficiency. Nothing could be less original than the mass communications aspect of this, the development and application of new techniques for the propagation–by both medium and message–of these so-called values. Nothing could be, in its real significance, more a gospel of stasis and rot.

Most dangerously, our idea of change is constructed such that it hides its worthlessness from the one who espouses it. Its self-defensive propaganda is a basic, ever-present part of its nature. If an adherent of technical newness has invented the next generation of software, then the automatic tendency of this "value" to present itself as the only value makes him accept that he has achieved all that "the new" or "change" can mean. In fact he has simply followed the drift of the present. He is effectively prevented by his intellectual formation from seeing that, in our time, the invention of software is exactly the sort of thing that is most imitative and repetitive, most worthless as a real departure from our routine notions and behaviors. In addition, this "inventor" will be greatly rewarded with attention and money, since the whole surrounding society upholds and swears by the same delusion. This will "change" his life in a technical sense. And this change-without-real-change will further make it impossible for him to see that to become successful for a variation of a nearly universal obsession is just a step in the current plod.

Our idea of newness and change is very antiquated, creaky, tired, monotonous, prosy, tedious, used up, redundant, timeworn. It is the dotage of an idea. In the era called the Enlightenment, approximately the 1700s, the idea was born that change is the basic nature of things, and is the supreme and maybe the only value. And in accord with this, the other idea was born of analyzing everything to understand it afresh but most importantly to get from it rational ways of making ourselves more and more powerful and wealthy. The name of these ideas came to be "revolution", and ever since then, "revolution" has been our chief cliché, and effectively our only concept. Each time and place tends to have its own forms of repetitiveness, its own forms of habitual action on which it prides itself though in fact they have become mere rigidity.

The characteristic rigor almost-mortis of our time is that technical change and the increasing production of wealth are still blessed as the new when they have long since become the repetition of a habit. For us, true change can only be to break free of "the new" as we now understand it.

The African slave trade was the irony of the Enlightenment ideas and preachings of human and civil rights. But it's also true that the African slave trade was perfectly in line with the more basic Enlightenment idea of applying rationalism to enterprise as to everything. Slavery by Europeans was not just an inconsistency with their new rational moral principles. More importantly, it was an effective action logically consonant with, and even recommended by, the rational approach to what we've come to call "the economy"–a statistically evaluated immense entity that corrupts the word used to name it, for "economy" translated plainly into the Queen's English means "good housekeeping".

As in those days, so today, civil and human rights seem more "rational" to many than the automatic action of "the economy" and the following out of whatever results from new economic rationalizations that statistics brand as improvements. However, the basic trend toward rationalization continues to be dominant socially, and to make the socially dominant procedure the seeking of rationally derived new methods and products. We still, massively, regard this as defining what is "new". We may in some sense–for practical purposes or to solace ourselves–"need" as-yet-uninvented technologies, pleasures, pop stars, tall buildings, resorts, investment vehicles, variations on the cellphone. But we must not continue to delude ourselves that there is or ever again can be any real newness in such things. On the contrary, creating them is the very essence of what, in our culture, is customary, tame, imitative, and without major value for an improved future. Their staleness guarantees that, given the actual difficulties we face, this approach cannot possibly yield any solution. It can only advance more new technical solutions, and the solutions cannot be technical.

In fact, the repetitively technical nature of our cultureless culture represents one of those adaptations of a species that is so successful that they become difficult to discard when the environment changes. Then, what had seemed to give strength becomes a threat of extinction, as the organism fails to alter its behavior for new circumstances. This can happen not only biologically but socially. We know of many examples. A good example for us to contemplate is the famous one of Rapa Nui / Easter Island. There, types of manufacture developed and mandated by an inflexible cultural tradition helped create disastrous deforestation, leading to overall environmental and social collapse. There was about an 80% decline in population over a century, and the rise of domination by warring strongman groups: gangs.

Burning all the trees is exactly what we are doing. It is exactly what modern technology automatically tends toward. Technology is our problem, the whole problem. Thus, in our case, it is technology–our adaptation, our technical approach to everything–that has actually created the menacing environment, which has become the menacing environment, that *is* the menacing environment, which it itself is hopelessly inadequate for adapting to. This is especially so when we understand the term technology as it should be understood: not just machines but rather the whole attitude of breaking everything down by rational analysis to create methods for building mechanisms for better outputs of efficiency, power and wealth. The smartest people ever born could think for a million years from within the methods of science and technology and they would never arrive–could never arrive–at the idea of diverting this technical approach from its rapacious course. It does not have within it any other value. It does not contain any source for a different view of life.

What we need, in fact, is the utter reorientation and the complete subordination of technical innovation and wealth-production under truly new, entirely different ideas. If there are to be any solutions to our problems of survival–and to social justice, and others–science and technology can only play a very subordinate and humble role. They can only be tools to help implement ways of seeing, living and working that come from elsewhere. They can help only if they are submitted to a general culture, to a whole and reasonable view of our existence.

The rationalizing procedure that is the very nature of all analytical approaches to knowledge is the opposite of reason. It actually "brackets out" wholeness. It "eliminates variables" for the sake of better calculation. Yet in all that truly concerns us, the whole subject is in the variables. When the question is humanity, society, and fullness of nature, it's a fine "science" that excludes the thing to be studied: the whole in its individual parts and persons, the unity "behind" things *only* in terms *of* the things. Rationalization is narrow focus to gain specific insights and turn them into methods for power. It's almost always destructive, even when not intentional. Reason is a total view of the situation we are concerned with, and the action of judgement in considering all its parts, determining what are leading factors and patterns, and thinking and deciding under the sign of the health of what we address. Reason alone deserves the honorable name of "intelligence". Not modern technological science or any of its works or accomplishments. As William of St. Thierry put it, "Amor ipse intellectus est": Love, in itself, is intellect.

Reason, a general culture, an intellectual procedure which always keeps first and foremost the view of the whole and the supreme reality and dignity of each individual person and thing: this is the source of the truly new, from the standpoint of our present methods and behaviors. And since we ought to have a brief, convenient and meaningful term to call it by, we might call it "poetry".

It would be right to name that which should govern our actions after its chief exemplar in human culture.

The Dearest Freshness Deep Down

Many poets and thinkers of the past have seen repetitiveness as an inescapable characteristic of existence: the wheel of the seasons, the wheel of fortune. The rigid deathliness and ruthless competitiveness of society, then, results from the human error of imitating rather than contradicting nature, which has this cyclical form. But perhaps we are unable to contradict nature, perhaps living and society-building necessarily copies it. In this view, the natural and social worlds as we find them are a limited and limiting environment which aware persons must either transform or escape by using the personal creativity that is uniquely human. Or they cannot transform and they cannot escape, and they must come to some spiritual accommodation with fate, using the power of moral wisdom that is uniquely human.

Other poets and thinkers have seen nature itself as the bearer of the new, which must be fulfilled in human beings. "There lives the dearest freshness deep down things", says Hopkins. We must rediscover the springs of nature–even the springs of nature that are beyond nature–and we must reconnect with the springs of ourselves. We must become again true to original innocence, in order to enact what nature really initiates...even, to enact what initiates nature itself, and ourselves with it. Nature in itself surges beyond itself, beyond its repetitions. Where and how it does this is in us, in having produced human beings. From this view the social perception that emerges is that many aspects of society, including some that seem most active, are petrified, because we have made the mistake of imitating only the self-perpetuation of nature and not its essence, which is its drive toward fulfillment, its spiritual thrust.

As I sat in my garden, hearing the news of the riot in Los Angeles among the flowering trees and plants in Toronto–where there was also a Rodney King riot, which like the LA riot mixed pure protests with youths carrying off VCRs and the like–I did not decide to my satisfaction whether the law of existence is an inescapable and collapsing cycle, or whether consciousness can transcend it, or whether the human person is thrust up by nature as nature's own possible self-completion. I did not figure out if all such ideas are the vain scrabblings after sense of an intelligent mouse in a very big maze, or if they are wonderful visions of a structure so vast and mysterious that it can be limitlessly re-envisioned, a world that is given to us for the joyful adventure of never-to-be-finished understanding.

The truth behind such musings is what the great primordial poets knew when they sang "of the wandering moon and the sun's bitter labors; where does the human race and where the animals come from, where do water and fire come from; ...why do the winter suns hurry so fast to dive into the ocean, or what is the delay that congeals the lingering nights". Such, Vergil tells us, was the poetry of "long-haired Iopas, he whom ancient Atlas taught", which is to say, the immemorial great poets of Africa. There was more than just an echo of them, there was a living continuation, in the street poet who had his moment on television during *Nightline*'s program. The essential and living rhythm of existence in its human form made itself heard briefly in a chant of protest and pride. In this poem, there were not exactly Iopas's cosmic flights, but there was the same authentic claim on the essential energy that existence gives to humankind. In this sense the cosmos was present and explained in the poem. "Every true poem," says Octavio Paz most truly, "no matter what its subject, is a model of the fraternity of the universe."

In that unruly poem existed a standard by which one could compare human impulses and works to separate those that tended toward a worthy fulfillment for men and women from those that spend our substance on self-distracting, self-defensive, self-destructive and other-destructive motives. Without songs like those of Iopas and the Los Angeles poet at its center, a city is empty, no matter how many busy people bustle under tall cranes raising a thousand walls.

And what is that standard? Wholeness. The wholeness, the simultaneous co-presence, of emotion and reason, of bodily experience and meditation, of memory and hope, defeat and unremitting aspiration, sorrow and joy. The fraternity of all things in the universe. The fraternity of all things in the universe of humanity.

The model of this: the poem.

Liberty or Death

A vast abstract painting bought for many thousands of dollars to provide the color scheme for a sixtieth-floor boardroom, and the chanting of pain and defiance to ABC's cameras by a street poet: both are flowerings of the energy that flows underground through the human, the American. But they are not equal or equivalent flowerings. The skyscraper and its contents, having been fed every richness, flourish easily; quite apart from anything that can worthily be called human consciousness, they serve the goal of maintaining and extending themselves. They produce a glorious spectacle, and can be contemplated and enjoyed. They belong not to the ones who plan and make them but to the ones who see and re-envision them, who walk among them, apparently small and marginal. "The great big city's a wondrous toy / Made for a girl and boy", said Lorenz Hart very truly. The great North American city centers are ours and we can revel in the growth of their splendor, if we wish, and in all the shoots and petals it puts forth: the Bugatti rushing by, the fashion model in full regalia being photographed by a plaza fountain as we pass, the film company on location, the Bösendorfer in a mansion's street-facing window, the buildings by Mies van der Rohe, the vast parklike wealthy neighborhoods where works of famous sculptors glisten, dampened by water sprinklers, amid backgrounds of golden chain laburnum, in front gardens behind black wrought-iron grilles.

All this rich variety of our cities is given to us exactly as seeds and berries are given to the birds, and to the ground, and to next spring. It belongs to those who see it, only secondarily to those who produce it. Actually, it's up to the seers to save the producers, or at least their products, or at least some value for their products. And these two categories of humans do not often overlap. To see the great city means to surmount and include it. To see in this sense means to acquire consciousness and self-consciousness, to be made human, and not simply to keep on making what you make for exterior motives. See truly, and henceforward you can never be merely a cog in the machine, though you cannot–to the appreciable extent that you are an expression of your environment–entirely separate yourself from it, either.

The riot and its poet are a very high-level flowering of the city, even though they spring up in supposedly poor soil. Few now are those with such a taste for true human energy that they can simply admire such manifestations of it as the riot. In many crucial respects, it is very difficult to do. There is no minimizing the beating of Reginald Denny, the 54 identified deaths and more than 2,000 injuries, the "more than $1 billion in damage", which statistic hides the many people deprived of jobs and homes in the destruction. I do not ignore that, if I had been present, my experience might have been that of Denny. Yet to value the riot is what we must try to do, and finally succeed in doing. It must be accepted with gratitude. Not just for its separable "positive" elements, but for the fullness of its reality.

For there, in its fullness, is the expression of the fact that everything human will flower, no matter how starved and repressed, and even in some cases twisted awry, or tragically bonded with its opposing evil, with self-thwarting and enraged resentment. Not "nevertheless" but because of this, the riot manifests that everything human will achieve expression. It manifests that the expression that humanity manages to find in dire circumstances will always be a demand for the means and freedom that permit *full* and *beautiful* expression. It will always mean this, despite the "negative" that hope's upthrust may damage, even break, the structures that repress it. We will always owe it our thanks. It alone absolves us, because it alone keeps putting in serious question the crime of our neglect and injustice, which otherwise would congeal into unspoken permanence. Everything human will flower because every person carries the human garden within him or her, and because all potentialities of the garden become greatest when they are most suppressed and threatened, as in our treeless ruinous stretches of square blocks where often the human person, impoverished and fed mainly with despair, is the only natural thing remaining.

The poet–the South Central Los Angeles poet and many other poets, in poverty and out of it–helps us. Through the poet, we can appreciate what the riot means. And through the poet, we could have the meaning and dispense with the riot, if only we were alert enough, attuned enough, to the poem. If we would only listen to the song of what the human being is and what it requires, and would grant those needs, would give an adequate outlet to those energies, they would not explode because of restriction. But restriction will fail, one way or another, against creative determination.

Since the powerful and wealthy and "competent", despite their longstanding failure in this regard, still think that their methods and ideas of change are what is needed, that only wealth can help the poor, that after all it is only wealth and power that the poor aspire to...let them think again. And completely differently. In fact the opposite is the case. If there is to be any future for wealth, if power is someday to cease being an ever-faster spinning of gears to nowhere or to the abyss, then it must resign its prestige, resign its control, and humbly serve what was expressed in South Central Los Angeles. It must listen and then serve, only serve. It must hope that what sprang up in South Central Los Angeles will never be diverted into American wealth's own repetitive, furiously dead methods, its patterns of self-indulgence and self-replication. Such a defeat of the riot's inner spirit would truly be the end of hope, the engulfment of the last human being by the living dead. Wealth and power and rationalistic technique must learn to hope that America will begin to be remade in some form truly different from their own, in some truly new image.

The present situation in the United States has many other possible outcomes, of course. I've been using metaphors–the flowering of human energy, the cycle and wheel of nature and of the technological society, and suchlike–and maybe I have not chosen the right metaphors, in the sense of the ones that are likely to become more and more determinant. For instance, I've only touched implicitly on a metaphor that is very powerful among us and once was explicit, although now it is rarely voiced: that the powerful are the fathers of the nation, and of the weak.

It is possible that the silencing of this metaphor, paternalism, by the intense criticism recently directed against it has only made it more effective. Never before has the United States as adamantly denied in word yet maintained in deed that the powerful will simply do whatever they want with the weak and their problems, whether by benevolently planning and directing from on high, or by exploiting, or by ignoring, or by studying and opining, or by applying the "philosophy" that their own success–the increase of the power of the powerful–will automatically, accidentally provide whatever the weak can validly ask for.

But it seems to me, considering metaphors such as paternalism, that we are always led back to the image of flowering, an authentic flowering of the essential human energy. For instance, if we consider any extended episode of comfortable fathers controlling and doling out what they please on behalf of their children, is the outcome ever anything but an equivalent of the South Central Los Angeles riot? There will always be an imposition on the children of a bogus and dispirited existence, and there will always be, at some point, at least here and there, a bursting forth of the authentic energy that will not be restrained or domesticated.

It's important to remember in this regard that the poet the riot put forward has many incarnations: he is not only that young African American chanting. He or she may also, for instance, speak to us through Czeslaw Milosz's inspired old age, as the great Polish poet, after a lifetime in the Augean stables of the twentieth century, turns his voice on paternalism and its laws:

> There is nothing to esteem in the fattened wisdom of adults, and acquiescence trained in slyness is disgraceful.
>
> Let us honor a protest against the immutable law and honor revolvers in the hands of adolescents when they refuse to participate forever.

In two lines of poetry, we are forcibly moved out of the rigidity of self-defensive authority and fear of life, and into the explosive revolt of a perpetual impulse for freedom which, if balked, will turn to refusal. "Give me liberty or give me death" runs one of the supposedly holy words of United States history. This is the human impulse, which *will* flower, in one way or another, creation or destruction, and which is always flowering in poetry.

Let's hope that, in our streets, things are not forced to the state Milosz mentions by those who want life to be the immutable law of their own concepts and eminence, and who try to freeze human energy into acquiescence for their own profit and security. But to avoid this fate, we must hear the street poet. We'll have to listen for the human energy where it is flowing healthfully "far above all will and authority and power and dominion". We'll have to realize and admit that the poet, and the people who know him and listen to him, are, immured in miserable streets with scarcely a tree, the human garden and its flourishing. These gardens exist still, but issue flames, not flowers, if the well-off will not abandon their selfish grasping–and restore and serve.

Coda in 1993

Now that no second South Central Los Angeles riot has followed the second trial of the officers who arrested Rodney King, we seem to be relaxing. Do we believe that these events are over? They won't be over for a long time yet.

Author's Afterword

The Garden was written in the late spring and early summer of 1992, after the Los Angeles jury verdict acquitting the police officers who had beaten Rodney King (3 March 1992), and the resulting unrest in South Central Los Angeles (29 April–5 May 1992). Its very short final coda was written after the second, federal court case (March 1993) in which two of the four officers were again acquitted of all charges, and the others were sentenced on some charges to thirty months imprisonment each. The book envisioned the long history and the constant repetition of such events, and so in a sense its subject was, already, the murder of George Floyd by police (25 May 2020) and the subsequent weeks of protests throughout the world. As the 1993 coda had said, such an event is profoundly one with the 1992 beating of Rodney King and the anti-injustice protests in South Central Los Angeles (now named South Los Angeles), as well as with the assassination of Martin Luther King (4 April 1968) and the following anti-racism violence in many U.S. cities.

In 1992-93 I did not try to publish *The Garden* mainly because of the energy-consuming nature of making ends meet, and partly because the essay was written as from an American. However, I've decided in light of recent events that I'd like to publish it. I was born in the U.S.A. and moved to Canada in late 1974. Like many immigrant Canadians, I retain a close interest in my country of origin. My interest in U.S. events and conditions was very close in 1992: indeed, it was still identification, substantial if not total. And my interest remains close now. So I have not varied my usage from the original writing, where "we" means "we Americans, including me, the author".

The root of my concern with racial injustice was my childhood reading of poetry, especially Blake and Whitman, plus my parents' activity for Black students in our local school systems, and for Black teachers and other workers. The earliest national event that galvanized me was the situation leading up to President Eisenhower's ordering of Federal troops to Little Rock, Arkansas, to safeguard the desegregation of Central High School. This was 1957; I was 10. But *The Garden* is more organically related to my university undergraduate years, 1965-1969.

In 1968, immediately after Dr. King's murder, I was flying home to Niles, Ohio, from Milwaukee: 12 April 1968. My university, Marquette University, provided a lengthy break at Easter, which that year was Sunday, 14 April. I was going to spend a couple of weeks at my job as an apprentice reporter for the Youngstown (Ohio) *Vindicator.* I flew over the rioting in Chicago, the smoke visible from the air. I arrived at the *Vindicator* to the furor of covering the rioting in the African American area of the city. As a cub, I was not sent there. I served as a rewrite man, typing the reporters' stories dictated by phone. I had just come from helping cover the days of steadily growing student protests at Marquette for the student newspaper, the Marquette *Tribune.* Soon, when I returned to campus, I would find myself both covering and joining in the student protests of that spring, which had become enormous and in which, for a time, all African American students withdrew from Marquette, charging "institutional racism". Massive sustained protests eventually forced university concessions. (I used to think of the fact that I entered university more or less simultaneously with the Watts Rebellion of August 1965, which had been occasioned by the police arrest of the 21-year-old Marquette Frye, and the subsequent violence of the police toward him, his brother, his mother, and others who gathered at the scene. Marquette Frye was a secret alternative namesake I could give the university in my thoughts.)

Since a key element of the essay portion of *The Garden* is the poem presented by a South Central Los Angeles poet, I want to say a few words about my relationship to this poem. I listened to the poem in the *Nightline* broadcast of 4 May 1992, as I was writing *The Garden*, prose and poetry, and wrote the essay portion based on my impression of the poem, confident that I could fill this in by obtaining a transcript. But repeated requests to ABC News, both in 1992-93 and in 2020, for a way to view the program or receive a transcript, were never answered.

So in 2020-2021 I also reached out to Los Angeles community–to the scholarly, the poetry, the journalistic, and the African American history communities. But very kind responses, including further organizations and persons to contact, and attempts by these helpers have not yielded the poet's identity. Among the people who have tried to help me, I must mention Professor Erna Smith, herself a former distinguished journalist who, when she was a Harvard University Fellow in the Shorenstein Center on Media, Politics and Public Policy produced the comprehensive investigation, "Transmitting Race: The Los Angeles Riot in Television News" (Discussion Paper Series #R-11, May 1994). Through Professor Smith I found *Nightline* alumni/ae to contact. Poets and publishers were especially generous in their attempts. I contacted poetry presses in Southern California (e.g. Angel City Press, Red Hen Press, others); individual members of the poetry and publishing community; Mr. Elias Wondimu, publisher and editorial director of TSEHAI publications at Loyola Marymount University–who connected me to Shonda Buchanan, editor of the two-volume poetry anthology *Voices from Leimert Park*, who in turn put me in touch with other local poets. But no one could remember or find the *Nightline* poet.

Then, at the suggestion of George Elliott Clarke, I made detailed queries to the Schomburg Center for Research in Black Culture of the New York Public Library. This was what finally paid off. Curator/librarian Shola Lynch recommended that I try the Vanderbilt University Television News Archive, in which it was possible, she said, the program in question is held. It is! Vanderbilt holds six *Nightline* programs, including four one-hour specials, from Los Angeles on the days of the uprising. Vanderbilt research librarian Nathan Jones reviewed the programs for me, located the poet, and helped me buy access to the program.

Alas, the poet remains unnamed. He was not identified by name during the program; the same was true for many of the community members who spoke. I do not know if he was a known poet in the community, or if he went on with poetry. Perhaps some day, even as the result of the publication of this book, I may still find out.

In 1992 I read the reportage and interpretations then written of the South Central Los Angeles uprising, and I've read later analyses in books and articles, and have watched the several excellent films on the subject. I've also become much more knowledgeable, since the early 1990s, about the poetic responses (still ongoing) to the unrest, not only from African American poets, but also from Latino and Korean poets, interested poets from unrelated groups, and rap artists and pop/folk artists. This material has let me add a few precisions to *The Garden* but it has not spurred any substantial critique of–rather, it has tended to parallel and reinforce–the book's central vision. So the poem remains as it was except for a couple of important additions, several minor ones, and some stylistic improvements. To be specific about additions, the material I added in 2020 is chiefly this author's note, and the substantial new writing necessary to place George Floyd in the poem's first part, "Three Kings: 1992, 1968, 2020". I've shortened the central part of the poem, about the marigold flower. Elsewhere there are small additions: for example, "Coda: The Zombies" now contains a reference to the collector's DVD edition of *The Night of the Living Dead* released in 1999. Such items are very few and brief.

Abundant poetry resulted from South Central in April-May 1992 and continues to be written, and there is much that I could put in dialogue with my poem by quotations and allusions of the type that are already numerous. But rather than rewriting to make such substitutions, I've preferred to stay with the original, powerful impression made on me by the street poet and his chanted poem on *Nightline*. This was a poem that had been created in and during the events, had been brought to television immediately afterwards, and was entirely of its time, without publication or recording or any presence in literary history or the histories of the events, as far as I can discover.

Both the poem and the essay portions of this book–the essay is just part of the poem–refer constantly to poetry. The African American poetry I have used is, generally, that of the Blues and other parts of the folk poetry tradition, and that of the preaching and speeches of Dr. King. The book-tradition poetry used is mainly non-African American; for instance, readers will notice Coleridge, Yeats, Whitman, and Blake. This is on purpose, i.e., it is an organic outcome of the poem's vision, one of whose dimensions is that great poetry is universally identical to the cry for justice of the poor and oppressed.

It happens that in April 2020, just before the murder of George Floyd, I published *As Far As You Know*, in which there is a poem, "Baltimore 2015", addressing the murder of Freddie Gray by Baltimore police (brutalized while under arrest, 12 April 2015; died, 19 April). In that poem, these lines occur:

> Last week they were burning Baltimore,
> the never solaced wound of the African
> never let heal, chains and bullets, the angry
> contentment of the others schooling themselves hard
> in the delusion: then is then and now is now.

The subject of *The Garden* is these murders and the outbursts against them: this rhythm. But its deeper subject is simply that of Doctor King and father Whitman: the poet's garden is the people. And the people are first of all the poor and excluded, for they are the closest to reality, and therefore the dearest–and especially dear to poetry, which is always travelling toward reality.

Poetry, the poor man's art, ever re-rooting itself in its garden, its people, its soil, its essential poverty.

Acknowledgments

I owe special thanks to my friends Ian Williams and George Elliott Clarke, who read this manuscript in 2020 as I was reviving and revising it, and offered detailed help, most of which I've incorporated. Their suggestions ranged from the title and subtitles, to important nuances and additions in phrasing for improved precision and clarity. Equally important suggestions for revision came from my editor and friend Shane Neilson, and Jeremy Luke Hill, the publisher of Gordon Hill Press and creator of the superb book and cover design. Of course, I owe great thanks, as mentioned above, to all who tried to help me find the *Nightline* South Central poet and his poem, and especially to George Elliott Clarke, Shola Lynch, and Nathan Jones, who finally let me see the poet and hear the poem after twenty-nine years, and transcribe it.

There are of course many allusions in the text to the Blues and popular music, to European, African, African American and other U.S. poetry, to oratory and preaching, and I do not wish to add apparatus identifying these. But I ought to state that the title "The Garden in the Midst" is taken from a great poem by Jorge Guillén, "Jardín en medio", in *Cántico*, and that cherishers of protest poetry will have noticed connections to Neruda's *Canción de gesta*: "song of war" or "epic song", and to Césaire's *Journal of a Return to the Native Land*.

About the Author

A. F Moritz's most recent books are *As Far As You Know* (2020), and *The Sparrow: Selected Poems* (2018), both from House of Anansi Press, and the 2015 re-publication by Princeton University Press of his 1986 volume, *The Tradition*. His twenty books of poetry have received such recognitions as the Griffin Poetry Prize, the Award in Literature of the American Academy of Arts and Letters, the Guggenheim Fellowship, and *Poetry* magazine's Bess Hokin Prize. Three of his books have been finalists for the Governor General's Award in Literature for poetry.